Just Beverly Cleary

by Charles Ricker

Harcourt
SCHOOL PUBLISHERS

All photos Harcourt.

Copyright © by Harcourt, Inc.

All rights reserved. No part of this publication may be reproduced or transmitted in any form or by any means, electronic or mechanical, including photocopy, recording, or any information storage and retrieval system, without permission in writing from the publisher.

Requests for permission to make copies of any part of the work should be addressed to School Permissions and Copyrights, Harcourt, Inc., 6277 Sea Harbor Drive, Orlando, Florida 32887-6777. Fax: 407-345-2418.

HARCOURT and the Harcourt Logo are trademarks of Harcourt, Inc., registered in the United States of America and/or other jurisdictions.

Printed in China

ISBN 10: 0-15-350524-9
ISBN 13: 978-0-15-350524-9

Ordering Options
ISBN 10: 0-15-350334-3 (Grade 4 Below-Level Collection)
ISBN 13: 978-0-15-350334-4 (Grade 4 Below-Level Collection)
ISBN 10: 0-15-357516-6 (package of 5)
ISBN 13: 978-0-15-357516-7 (package of 5)

If you have received these materials as examination copies free of charge, Harcourt School Publishers retains title to the materials and they may not be resold. Resale of examination copies is strictly prohibited and is illegal.

Possession of this publication in print format does not entitle users to convert this publication, or any portion of it, into electronic format.

4 5 6 7 8 9 10   0940   12 11 10 09

Beverly Cleary loved books. She read a lot when she was a child. When she was in third grade, the librarian at her school told Beverly something important. She told Beverly that she should write books for children when she got older.

Beverly liked that idea. She decided that one day she would write good books for children. She did it! Beverly grew up to become one of the most brilliant and successful children's book writers of all time!

Beverly Cleary was born in 1916, in McMinnville, Oregon. She lived with her parents on a farm near Yamhill, Oregon. Young Beverly loved stories. She often asked her mother to tell her stories. The small town of Yamhill, however, did not have a public library. Beverly's mother had books from the state library sent to Yamhill. That way Beverly's mother had many books to read to her daughter.

Beverly's family did not have a lot of money. When Beverly was six years old, her family moved to Portland, Oregon. These were hard times. Beverly's parents urged her to remember her ancestors. They were pioneers. Beverly's parents said that pioneers had hard lives, but they survived.

Beverly enjoyed Portland. She really liked the public library there. Beverly and her mother went to the library every week. They would check out books. Beverly read many books. She wondered why there weren't more books about everyday children like her.

Beverly completed high school. She went to college, and she graduated in 1938. She learned to be a librarian. She became the children's librarian at a public library. The library was in Yakima, Washington.

Beverly worked with many children there. She read them many books. Some of the children complained about the books. They said there weren't many "books about kids like us."

Beverly got married in 1940. She married a man named Clarence. Soon after, the United States entered World War II. Beverly wanted to help her country. She worked at an army hospital in California. She was the librarian there.

When World War II ended, Beverly and Clarence bought a house in California. Beverly found some writing paper in one of the closets. When she saw the writing paper, she knew it was time for her to start writing!

Beverly decided to write a book. Then she remembered the children in Yakima. She thought about the kinds of books they might enjoy. Her first book was about a boy named Henry Huggins.

Henry is an everyday boy. He feels like nothing interesting ever happens to him. Then he meets a stray dog named Ribsy. A stray dog is one without an owner. After he meets Ribsy, Henry's life changes. He finds himself participating in all kinds of great adventures. The book was titled *Henry Huggins*. It was published in 1950. Beverly was now an author!

Beverly continued to write books. She wrote *Ellen Tebbits* in 1951. This funny book is about Ellen and her friend. Ellen is a third grader.

Another book Beverly wrote about Henry Huggins is called *Henry and Ribsy*. This funny book is about when Henry tried to train his dog Risby.

Beverly became the mother of twins. They were a boy and a girl, and she named them Marianne and Malcolm. Beverly would later write a book about twins. The book was called *Mitch and Amy*, and it was based on her children.

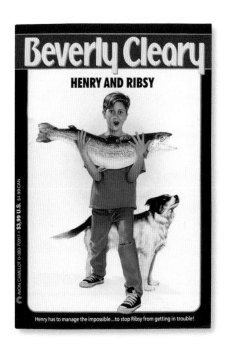

Beverly's books are about everyday life. They are about regular people. The books are not set in exotic places. Instead, they take place in regular places.

The artists that draw the pictures make the people look like regular people, too. They wear clothes that regular people wear. Sometimes their hair is even a little bit messy!

Beverly's mother gave her advice. She said, "Make your writing funny. People always like to read something funny. Also, keep it simple. The best writing is simple writing." Beverly followed her mother's advice. Her books are funny and simple. That is why so many children enjoy them.

Beverly created a girl named Ramona Quimby. She is one of Beverly's most famous characters. Ramona is the mischievous sister of Beezus. Beverly first wrote about Ramona in her Henry Huggins books. Then Ramona got her own books. The first was *Beezus and Ramona*. Beverly wrote that one in 1955.

Ramona does not go through life gracefully. She gets in trouble. She makes bad decisions. She gets frustrated. She is just like people in real life. That is probably why so many people enjoy reading about her. Beverly wrote eight Ramona Quimby books.

One time, Beverly's son did not feel well. Beverly gave him a toy motorcycle. He played with the toy a lot. That gave Beverly an idea. She began to write about a special mouse named Ralph S. Mouse. In *The Mouse and the Motorcycle*, Ralph the mouse and a boy become good friends. The boy lets Ralph ride his toy motorcycle. She wrote two more books about Ralph. They are called *Ralph S. Mouse* and *Runaway Ralph*.

Beverly wrote more than thirty-five books over the years. She won many awards for her writing. She won the Newbery Medal in 1984, for her book *Dear Mr. Henshaw*. This is an award for the best children's book of the year. She has sold millions of copies of her books. Her books are sold in twenty different countries! Some of her books have even been made into television shows.

The city of Portland honored Beverly in 1995.
That is when the Beverly Cleary Sculpture Garden
for Children opened. The garden is in a park. It has
sculptures of some of Beverly's book characters.
There are sculptures of Henry Huggins and
Ramona Quimby. In one of the sculptures, Ramona
is smiling. In the other she is grumpy. An artist
named Lee Hunt did the sculptures. Beverly Cleary
thought that this artist understood her characters
very well!

Beverly wrote two books about her amazing
life. She wrote *A Girl from Yamhill* in 1988. She
wrote *My Own Two Feet* in 1995.

Think Critically

1. Does the author think Beverly's books are funny? Is that a fact or an opinion?

2. What is one reason that Beverly decided to write funny books?

3. What important event happened to Beverly in the third grade?

4. How would you describe most of the characters in Beverly Cleary's books?

5. What did you learn from this book?

 Art

Character Picture Draw a picture of your favorite Beverly Cleary character. Then write three words under the picture that tell about that character.

 **School-Home Connection** Share this book with a family member. Then have a discussion about what kinds of stories you enjoy.